LATINOS IN BASEBALL

Bernie Williams

Carrie Muskat

Mitchell Lane Publishers, Inc.
P.O. Box 619
Bear, Delaware 19701

LATINOS IN BASEBALL

Tino Martinez	Bobby Bonilla	Roberto Alomar	Pedro Martinez
Moises Alou	Sammy Sosa	Ivan Rodriguez	**Bernie Williams**
Ramon Martinez	Alex Rodriguez	Vinny Castilla	Manny Ramirez

Second Printing
Library of Congress Cataloging-in-Publication Data

Muskat, Carrie
    Bernie Williams / Carrie Muskat.
        p. cm. — (Latinos in baseball)
    Includes index.
    Summary: A biography of the New York Yankee center fielder, Bernie Williams, winner of the 1998 American League batting title.
    ISBN 1-58415-011-4
    1. Williams, Bernie, 1968—Juvenile literature. 2. Baseball players—Puerto Rico—Biography—Juvenile literature. [1. Williams, Bernie, 1968- 2. Baseball players. 3. Puerto Ricans—Biography.] I. Title. II. Series.

GV865.W48 M78 2000
796.357'092—dc21
[B]   99-053141

About the Author: Carrie Muskat has covered major league baseball since 1981, beginning with United Press International in Minneapolis. She was UPI's lead writer at the 1991 World Series. A freelance journalist since 1992, she is a regular contributor to *USA Today* and *USA Today Baseball Weekly*. Her work has appeared in the *Chicago Tribune, Inside Sports,* and *ESPN Total Sports* magazine. She is the author of several baseball books for children, including *Barry Bonds* (Chelsea House), *Sammy Sosa* (Mitchell Lane), *Moises Alou* (Mitchell Lane), and *Mark McGwire* (Chelsea House).

Photo Credits: cover: ©1999 New York Yankees; pp. 4, 6, 15, 27 ©1999 New York Yankees; p. 36 Stephen Dunn/Allsport; p. 37 Doug Pensinger/Allsport; p. 43 Mike Segar/Archive Photos; pp. 47, 65 ©1999 New York Yankees.

Acknowledgments: The following story was developed based on personal interviews with Bernie Williams on May 21, 22, and 23, June 18 and 19, and July 27, 28, and 29, 1999. Professional and personal friends and family members were also interviewed for this book. This story has been thoroughly researched and checked for accuracy. To the best of our knowledge, it represents a true story. The author and publisher gratefully acknowledge the cooperation and helpfulness of Bernie Williams and the New York Yankees in the development of this book.

Mitchell Lane
PUBLISHERS

TABLE OF CONTENTS

CHAPTER ONE
Batting Champion

On September 27, 1998, a rowdy crowd of 49,608 was packed into Yankee Stadium to watch their beloved New York Yankees play the last game of the regular season. The unlucky opponents were the Tampa Bay Devil Rays, an expansion team just completing its first year.

It had been an incredible season for the Yankees, who were fondly known as the Bronx Bombers. The Yankees had won the American League East Division nearly three weeks earlier on September 9 with a 7-5 victory over their rivals, the Boston Red Sox. It was New York's seventh division title and the earliest since divisional play began in 1969.

The final regular-season game gave the Yankees a chance to set the bar higher in the baseball record books. The record for most wins in a single season was 111, set by the 1954 Cleveland Indians. Entering the final regular-season game, the Yankees had won 113 games. They wanted to make it 114.

It had been a season of high expectations. The Yankees had taken over sole possession of first place on April 21, 1998, and had stayed there for the rest of the season—a total of 159 consecutive days. They had a 22-game lead over the Red Sox on the final day, and Boston had the second-best record in the American League.

Bernie Williams, the Yankees' talented center fielder, came into the season finale as the top hitter in the league, leading Boston's Mo Vaughn by a few percentage points. Yankees manager Joe Torre knew how close the race for the batting title was. All of New York knew what was at stake.

Williams collected two hits in two at-bats in the game to raise his average to .339. In the sixth inning, Torre called the stadium press box from the dugout phone. The Red Sox had just finished playing the Baltimore Orioles at Fenway Park in Boston, and Torre wanted to know how Vaughn had done. The report was that the big first baseman had had two hits in his four at-bats to post a .337 average. Now Torre knew. Bernie Williams had won the American League batting title.

Torre pulled Bernie from the game. A couple extra innings' rest could only benefit the player and the Yankees as they looked ahead to the playoffs.

Bernie hit .339 in 1998 to capture the American League batting title.

Bernie went to the clubhouse and took off his pin-striped jersey before heading to the weight room to work out. But before he could get started, teammate David Wells stopped him. The Yankee Stadium scoreboard had flashed that Bernie had won the batting title, and the fans were on their feet, cheering and calling for him to take a curtain call. The game was not going to continue until Williams obliged the crowd.

Wearing a navy T-shirt and his shower slippers, Bernie walked down the narrow tunnel that leads from the Yankees' clubhouse to the dugout and stepped to the top of the steps to wave to the appreciative fans. It was a moment he cherished.

Williams was now ranked among baseball's best. He was the first Yankee to win the batting title since Paul O'Neill had done so in 1994 when he hit .359. Don Mattingly had preceded O'Neill, hitting .343 to claim the 1984 title.

"It really shows that you're the top player that particular year," Williams said. "Only so many guys have the opportunity to go for the batting title in the big leagues. It sort of sets you apart from the whole crowd of players. Once you win a batting title, it says, 'This guy is in a select group.' You want the respect from your peers and coaches and people around the league. Winning one of these certainly sets you apart."

"He's the type of guy who, when he gets into a groove, he doesn't lose it," said Yankees hitting coach Chris Chambliss. "That's a tribute to his hard work and [keeps] him aggressive.

"It's not that he gets lazy," Chambliss said, "but he gets deliberate about things and sometimes that slows him down. Once he knows that he's doing well and he feels it—I don't know what it is but a certain surge within him that he understands that everything is OK and he feels good about it—that's when he takes off. When he does that, he stays that way for a long time. That contributes to winning a batting title. He just gets hot."

The Yankees won their final regular-season game 8-3 against Tampa Bay and clinched a 114-48 record. They had shattered the club record of 110 wins set by the 1927 Yankees, a powerful team that had boasted a lineup nicknamed Murderers' Row because of sluggers Babe Ruth and Lou Gehrig.

Winning the batting title wasn't Bernie Williams' only accomplishment in 1998. The Yankees would go on to great things in the postseason. But that year, Bernie also discovered what a unique individual he was. And it had nothing to do with hitting a fastball or making a great running catch.

CHAPTER TWO
"Verde Luz"

The island of Puerto Rico is located in the Caribbean Sea southeast of Florida's southernmost tip. Its name means "Rich Harbor," and it measures roughly 100 miles east to west and 35 miles north to south. There are miles and miles of beautiful beaches around the coastline, and the climate is perfect for baseball.

Baseball is believed to have been introduced to Puerto Rico during the Spanish-American War in 1898. Today, it is the most popular game on the island. Children play year-round, either in youth leagues or on their own in the streets and parks.

The first Puerto Rican to make it to the big leagues was pitcher Hi Bithorn. He pitched primarily for the Chicago Cubs and won 18 games in 1943 before leaving for World War II. Vic Power became the first Puerto Rican to play in a major-league All-Star Game, doing so in 1955. He played from 1954 to 1965 and compiled a .284 career average.

One of the most revered players to come from Puerto Rico was outfielder Roberto Clemente, who starred in the big leagues with the Pittsburgh Pirates. Clemente batted .317 over 18 seasons (1955–72) with the Pirates. He reached 3,000 hits on the last day of the 1972 season. On New Year's Eve 1972, he was killed in a plane crash on a mercy mission to earthquake victims in Nicaragua. Clemente was elected to baseball's Hall of Fame by a special vote the next year.

Every Puerto Rican knows about Clemente. Most players old enough can remember where they were the day he died. Families pass on the story from generation to generation. The news shocked the tiny island.

One of Puerto Rico's early baseball heroes was Irmo Figueroa, a terrific hitter who played in the 1959 Pan Am Games for Puerto Rico. "Irmo Figueroa was like Babe Ruth to amateur baseball in Puerto Rico," said Luis Mayoral, a Puerto Rican broadcaster with the major-league Texas Rangers.

Irmo's brother, Jedan Figueroa, was a catcher and also played professional baseball in Puerto Rico in the late 1950s and early '60s. He made the spring roster for the Washington Senators but returned to Puerto Rico, uncomfortable with the severity of racism in those days.

Irmo and Jedan were the uncles of Bernabe Figueroa Williams (b. September 13, 1968), who is better known as Bernie Williams. Baseball was in Bernie's genes.

Bernie's family lived in Vega Alta, a town located about a half-hour drive west of the capital city of San Juan. At the age of eight, Bernie, who was the oldest of two sons of Bernabe and Rufina Williams, could play the guitar. His favorite song was a Puerto Rican folk song called "Verde Luz," or "Green Light," which was about the island's beautiful beaches and mountains. It was at this age that the youngster became interested in baseball, although he did so somewhat reluctantly.

Bernie's mother thought her children were spending too much time inside watching television, so she told them to go outside and play. That's when Bernie discovered baseball. It was the start of a long and wonderful friendship.

Bernie was taller than other kids his age. "People were asking all the time if he was older than the rest of us," said Jose Hernandez, an infielder with the Chicago Cubs who grew up with Bernie in Vega Alta. "He was strong and huge compared to everybody else."

Children played pickup baseball games on the streets and in the parks, using tennis balls or rubber balls and tree branches for bats. As soon as school let out, kids would run to their favorite makeshift diamonds to play. "Anything we could hit with, we'd use," Hernandez said. "Every day, somebody would bring something new." Sometimes kids would use plastic bottle caps as baseballs, throwing them like Frisbees to the hitters. Jose used to wear jeans with extra knee pads because of all the sliding he did playing baseball.

Bernie attended a private school while Hernandez went to a public school in Vega Alta. But they saw each other a lot on the baseball diamonds. "He was tall and we were so short. He was always bigger than the other kids," Hernandez said of Bernie. "He could run, he could hit. He was fast—he was always safe at first."

Williams *was* fast. He was a member of his school's track team and had blazing speed. He would also go to the playground with his father. The elder Williams would watch as his son swung hand over hand on the monkey bars to build up his upper-body strength.

Bernie's mother was a schoolteacher, and education was very important to her and her family. Bernie was schooled in more than just reading and writing. His musical talents were exceptional, and at the age of 13 he received a scholarship to attend the Escuela Libre de Musica, a school that had an extensive music program for students in seventh to twelfth grades. Bernie studied math and literature, too, but he was most often seen with his guitar, playing classical or jazz music in the hallways.

He still enjoyed athletics, and, at the age of 15, he won four gold medals at an international track meet. Bernie was ranked among the top 400-meter runners in his age group.

Juan Gonzalez, the two-time American League MVP with the Texas Rangers, grew up in nearby Vega Baja. He had been a teammate of Williams' in the youth baseball league. Williams had the speed while Gonzalez had the power. They played outfield on the same "Mickey Mantle" team at Clemente Sports City, a complex named after the late Puerto Rican Hall of Famer. Major-league teams often had scouts at the center to keep an eye out for young talent.

Julio Navarro, a former big-league pitcher whose son Jaime Navarro played in the major leagues with the Milwaukee Brewers, Chicago Cubs and Chicago

White Sox, was among those watching young Williams on the playing field.

"That guy is going to make it in the big leagues," Julio told Jaime.

In the summer of 1985, when Bernie was 16 years old, Roberto Rivera, a scout for the New York Yankees, was at the Clemente Sports City complex, the "mecca for juvenile baseball." Rivera was actually interested in Gonzalez, who was playing right field. Bernie was in center. Between innings, the loudspeakers would play lively salsa music. Gonzalez loved the Latin rhythm, and he danced in the outfield to the music.

Williams remembers falling as a fly ball went over his head, then scrambling to his feet and quickly recovering it. Rivera was more impressed with Williams' footwork and athletic ability than Gonzalez's dance steps. The scout recommended the Yankees sign the young center fielder. Fred Ferreira, who was the Yankees' head scout in Latin America, agreed after seeing Williams play just once.

"My eyes were really focused on Bernie," said Ferreira, who became the director of international operations for the Montreal Expos. "He showed me a lot of ability."

Williams was not yet 17—his birthday was September 13—which is the legal age for players to sign professional baseball contracts, so the Yankees had to do something. The team assigned Williams to a baseball camp in Connecticut. "We had to hide him for six months," Ferreira said, to try to keep his prize out of sight of other big-league scouts.

Bernie had considered attending the University of Puerto Rico. He had been offered a scholarship and wanted to study to become a doctor. His mother and father were eager to see him pursue such a challenging and rewarding field as medicine.

Bernie knew school would always be there. How long would he be able to take advantage of his athletic skills? He decided to put school on hold and pursue a career in baseball.

He did keep his guitar. "From ninth [grade] to senior year, I learned to play the basics while still playing baseball," Williams said about his music. "But then it came time for me to choose between baseball and music, and I decided to take my swings. I can always go back to music, but I can only play baseball while I'm still young."

He was familiar with the New York Yankees. In 1978, Puerto Ricans were talking about pitcher Ed Figueroa, who became the first Puerto Rican to win 20 games in a major-league season. Bernie was more interested in the Yankees hitters of that era: Reggie Jackson, Chris Chambliss and Willie Randolph.

"I was one of those 'playoff fans.' When teams got up to the final moments of the season, it got my attention," said Williams, who didn't really follow one team. "In 1977 and '78, I was fortunate enough to watch the World Series with the Yankees and Reggie and Bucky Dent and Graig Nettles and Chambliss and Willie."

Little did he know then that someday he would wear the same pinstripes and have Chambliss and Randolph as his coaches.

Bernie's parents gave him their blessing. It was time to see what he could do.

The No. 5 on Bernie's sleeve is for Yankee legend Joe DiMaggio.

CHAPTER THREE
Ready to Play

Bernie Williams' professional career officially started in 1986 in Sarasota, Florida, for the New York Yankees Gulf Coast League team. Fred Ferreira, the scout who first signed Williams, was his manager. "We did everything we could to utilize his speed," said Ferreira of Williams, who stole 33 bases that year. He batted .270 and was named to the league's All-Star team.

That winter, Williams returned home to Puerto Rico and was a reserve outfielder for the talented Caguas Criollos team. It was hard to break into the Criollos lineup because of the outfielders already there, including future major-leaguers Ellis Burks and Henry Cotto. Williams had practiced with the 1985–86 team and was treated well by the big-leaguers. Ivan Calderon, who would play for the Chicago White Sox and Seattle Mariners, even gave the youngster one of his gloves.

Tim Foli was the Caguas manager in 1986–87 and could tell that Williams was special even at a young age.

"He was a very educated boy and it was kind of neat because at first, he was out of place," Foli said. "He really wasn't used to the rigamarole of baseball. He was more of a laid-back person. He had a whole lot of raw ability."

Foli was impressed by Williams' speed and his arm. They worked on bunting and base stealing. "He wanted to learn," Foli said. "He had the tools. He just didn't know how to use many of them at that time."

Williams was an eager student.

"He responded well to coaching," Foli said. "He could take it in and respond positively to it. You knew the kid was going to develop. It was just important that nobody threw him into the fire too quick and that he got a chance to use those tools and develop. He's always been very durable and he takes care of himself. He's just a sharp kid and he's got his priorities straight."

Foli and his wife enjoyed their winter in Puerto Rico. One of Bernie's teammates was Roberto Alomar, and the young players often went to the Folis' house for dinner. "We had our family there and it was like they were our other adopted children," Foli said.

But the manager discovered how important winning is in Puerto Rico. Caguas hit eight home runs but lost 14-13 to the Dominican team in one game of the 1987 Caribbean World Series. The Criollos management replaced Foli with coach Ramon Aviles. Caguas went on to win four straight games to earn the title.

As Foli reflected on the incredible talent he had that one season, he said he felt lucky to be part of their development.

"They were just babies and you knew they had the ability," he said. "It was really neat to me because they've turned out to be great human beings, too. It's nice they have all that money but they still realize how important family is and how they're supposed to treat people. They always have and they always will."

Foli could tell that both Williams and Alomar had come from good families and had been taught to respect authority and their elders. They also had respect for the game.

"Bernie understood what he had to do to be successful," Foli said. "Because he gave himself a good foundation, he was able to let his tools take over. The way he's taken care of his life, not only is he a great baseball player, but he's a great man. That's kind of special."

When Foli returned to the United States, he phoned Yankees owner George Steinbrenner and personally told him how special Williams was and that it was important to give the youth time to develop. That's exactly what the Yankees did.

Williams split the next season, 1987, between the Yankees' Class-A teams in Ft. Lauderdale and Oneonta. He suffered a separated shoulder on May 7, which sidelined him for one month. When he was healthy, he reported back to Oneonta and batted .344 in 25 games. A groin pull later that year limited his playing time, but the Yankees front office had seen enough. On November 18, 1987, the team added Williams to its 40-man roster.

Williams played for Class A Prince William in 1988 and batted .335 until his season ended July 14, when he ran into an outfield wall at Hagerstown chasing a fly ball. A fractured right wrist sidelined him for the remainder of the year. Despite ending his season early, he still led the Carolina League in hitting.

When Bernie returned to Puerto Rico that winter, he and his brother Hiram went to play some playground baseball. Hiram stopped Bernie before he could take a swing.

"He said, 'You can't play against me from the right side now because you're a pro, so you've got to switch,'" Bernie said. "So I started hitting the ball from the left side."

The Yankees coaches had only seen Bernie hit right-handed. When he reported to spring training camp in 1989, he felt comfortable enough to show off his switch-hitting abilities. During batting practice before the Grapefruit League games started, Bernie asked one of the coaches if he could bat left-handed. Sure, the coach said. Williams stepped to the plate with the bat poised over his left shoulder.

"I started hitting rockets," Williams said. "All of that practice had paid off."

Buck Showalter was the Yankees' Class-A manager, and Williams was to be his center fielder. Bernie asked Showalter if he could continue to practice batting left-handed as well as right-handed, and Showalter encouraged him. Good switch-hitters are a luxury for a team, and Bernie had definitely improved his value to the Yankees.

"There were a few times when Bernie wanted to drop it but he kept with it," Showalter said. "His age was in his favor and he was such a good athlete. He was such an artistic, athletic guy that he had switch-hitter written all over him. A lot of young kids that are 18 or 19, as soon as they have some failure from that other side they really start fighting it because they know that at this level they can do well batting from one side. I was thinking down the road when he gets where the breaking balls are better, what a weapon it would be for him to be a switch-hitter."

Showalter had a few other players try to hit from both sides. "For every success like Bernie, there were a few failures, too," he said.

Williams was an easy player to coach. "I could never get mad at Bernie," Showalter said. "You just trusted his skills. His instincts came with playing time. He was very intelligent. He came from a great family. He was well educated. Bernie would've been successful at anything he did. He had a passion for success and he didn't mind working."

Williams played for both Class AAA Columbus and Class AA Albany in 1989. He hit a combined .239 with 13 homers and 58 RBIs. Before he spent the next year in Albany, Bernie married Waleska in February 1990. That season he batted .289 with eight homers and 54 RBIs. He also led the Eastern League with 39 stolen bases. *Baseball America* magazine named him to its Class AA All-Star team and listed him as the second-best prospect in the entire Eastern League.

The following season Williams was on the Class AAA Columbus roster. On July 7, 1991, he got the phone call every minor-league player dreams of. The Yankees needed him. It was time to go to the big leagues. Yankees' center fielder Roberto Kelly had suffered a sprained wrist when he ran into a fence chasing a ball, and the team needed a replacement. The 22-year-old

Williams was inserted into the starting lineup that day, the last before the All-Star break, and made the most of his debut with a sacrifice fly, an infield single and two RBIs against the Baltimore Orioles. The infield single was his first major-league hit, and it came in the ninth inning off Orioles closer Gregg Olson.

Williams started the next 20 games in July for the Yankees. In the first 10 games, he batted .355, but then he went 7 for 40 (.175) over the next 10 games. In his fifth game and 16th at-bat, Williams hit his first major-league home run, connecting off California's Chuck Finley.

The Yankees liked what they saw. Williams started all 31 of New York's games in August. He experienced the highs and lows of the game very early. He put together a seven-game hitting streak from July 31 to August 6, but on August 21 at Kansas City, he struck out all five times he went to the plate. The only other Yankee to do that was pitcher Johnny Broaca on June 25, 1934.

On August 28, Williams hit his first left-handed homer against Texas' Wayne Rosenthal. Bernie struggled that September, batting just .186, but he finished strong with a .409 average in the last six games, including a five-hit game October 5 against the Cleveland Indians. Roberto Kelly, whom Williams had replaced in the lineup when Kelly was hurt, had also posted a five-hit game earlier that season.

Bernie had to deal with more than big-league pitching. A few of the Yankee players teased him, thinking he was too soft to make it in the big leagues. Williams had a wide-eyed look and was very quiet and kept to himself. The older players nicknamed him Bambi. They taunted him mercilessly.

"I don't know who it was, but it was a great philosopher who said, 'What doesn't kill you makes you stronger.' That's the way I took it," Williams said. "It's very important to never give up and have a lot of confidence in your abilities to do whatever it is that you're doing and not let anybody get you down or put you down. I think that's the most important thing, especially in this line of work. If you don't have confidence in your ability, the battle is half lost. There's competition from everybody—from the opposition to the people who are trying to get your job. There is such a lot of competition and hard-hitting feelings from people around you, [even] people who call themselves teammates. There's a lot to be said for camaraderie."

Williams talked to his family for support. He never let the bullies get the best of him.

"I didn't want to give up my dream," Bernie said. "The time that I was here, I realized I'd worked so hard in the minor leagues to try to get up to this level that I was not going to let something as trivial as that—even though, at the time, it was not—in any way interfere with my goal, which was to establish myself as a major-league baseball player."

While Williams was courageous against the teasing, he also got a boost from another veteran player, Don Mattingly. Mattingly was a throwback to the Yankees players of the past. He wore the pinstripes from 1982 to 1995, and wore them proudly. When Mattingly retired after the 1995 season, Williams lobbied for Mattingly's corner locker in the Yankee Stadium clubhouse. The space is special to Bernie.

Mattingly did what he could to help Williams deal with his mean-spirited teammates.

"He did as much as he could without making it look too obvious," Bernie said of Mattingly. "He was one of the few guys who respected me as a player when I first came in. Whatever potential I had, he saw it. He really wanted me to do good. He was just great."

One night, while the Yankees were riding from a stadium to a hotel after a road game, Mattingly steered Williams to the back of the bus. He wanted a private word with the young outfielder. "He told me, 'You know you're good. You're a good player but you need to work on this and this and this,'" Williams said of his conversation with the Yankees captain. "He was telling me the things I was good at and the things I needed to work on to be a better player. I was so overwhelmed that it was him who was telling me and not a coach or the general manager. It was my teammate—and what a teammate. The captain of the club. It was just a great experience for me."

Bernie started the 1992 season on the Yankees' 25-man major-league roster, but he played in just two games. On April 15 he was optioned to Class AAA Columbus. It was a difficult assignment to accept, especially after getting a taste of the big league.

"I had made the team out of spring training," Williams said, "and about a week after the season was under way, the manager called me to his office and told me, 'You're not going to be a player who will be playing every day here. You're young, so it's not going to be of any benefit to you to be here and stay on the bench as a role player, playing defense once in a while or pinch-hitting or pinch-running. Since you have all this potential and you're young, you can refine your skills and play on a daily basis in the minors.'

"It was kind of discouraging," Bernie said, "because I was looking forward to making the club. But at the same time, it was not going to do me any good to be in the big leagues and play part-time. I felt that it would be more frustrating for me to stay up and not play."

His minor-league assignment did not last the season. Williams was called back to the big-league team on July 31 to replace injured Yankee outfielder Danny Tartabull. On August 1, Williams was inserted into the lead-off spot, and he started every game the rest of the season.

He also was reunited with Mattingly, who helped him learn the Yankee way. "He was one of the players I had the pleasure to watch as he went about his business on the field," Williams said of the man known as Donnie Baseball. He said Mattingly gave him some advice: "He told me one thing: 'Whatever you do, just come here ready to play every day.' Up to this day, it's a great piece of advice that I keep. He taught me how to do that.

"I think that's one of the differences between great players and players who are good and players who are not consistent," Williams continued. "The ability that they have to be prepared mentally on a daily ba-sis—that's one of the toughest things to do for me as a player, to be there mentally. I know that physically I'm not going to be there all of the time. Your body breaks down, you get hurt, this and that, you're not going to feel good all the time. But mentally, that's one of the things you can control. It is tough at times. People who are able to put it in gear and kick themselves in the rear end once in a while and make sure they're ready to per-form up to their level when it's asked for—I think that's what separates great players from the ones who are not."

It was an important lesson to learn at a young age.

CHAPTER FOUR
The Yankee Way

There would be no shuttling between minor-league teams in Columbus or Albany for Bernie Williams in 1993. He was in the major leagues to stay.

He had several new teammates on the 1993 Yankees. Outfielder Paul O'Neill, hitting specialist Wade Boggs and left-handed pitcher Jimmy Key joined Williams in manager Buck Showalter's lineup that year. Williams started the season as the lead-off hitter and batted .239 in 66 starts. But Showalter decided to change his lineup after the All-Star break and dropped Williams to the No. 6 spot. This way, Bernie would have more opportunities to drive runners in. The move paid off as Williams batted .373 with 10 RBIs in the first 15 games and posted a .298 average after the break.

In his first full season, Williams put together a 21-game hitting streak in August, the longest by a Yankee since Don Mattingly hit safely in 24 straight games in 1986.

Injuries hindered Williams the following spring. He struggled with a sore shoulder and a groin pull, and when the regular season got under way, Bernie was hitting just .168 on May 9. Two days later, he snapped an 0-for-18 slump against Cleveland with an RBI single in the fifth inning off Dennis Martinez, and then he took off. Bernie hit .326 the rest of the season.

Williams may have gotten off to a slow start, but the Yankees did not. The talent-loaded team had a 25-10 record by May 15 and was posting dramatic, come-from-behind wins. O'Neill was carrying the team with a major-league leading .461 average.

"It's a great feeling," Yankees outfielder Danny Tartabull said. "Every day you come out to win that particular day. It feels good when you do. This game is not going to allow you to do that every night. But we're going to keep trying."

Williams started the month of June hitless in the first three games and then put together one of the best three-game stretches of any Yankee all season. From June 6 to 8 at Texas, he homered in three straight games for the first time in his career and went 7 for 12 with two doubles, four homers and 11 RBIs.

Bernie is a dangerous hitter from both sides of the plate.

The big day was June 6. On that day, Bernie homered from both sides of the plate, the fifth Yankee switch-hitter to do so. Among the other Yankees who have accomplished the feat was the legendary Mickey Mantle, who did so 10 times.

Bernie's average increased each month. He hit .178 in April, .282 in May, .316 in June, .327 in July and .327 in August. But the 1994 season abruptly ended on August 12 because of a labor dispute between baseball's owners and the players union. The players strike resulted in the cancellation of the remainder of the season, including the postseason and the World Series.

A settlement was reached for the 1995 season, and Williams reported, ready to go. Again, he got off to a slow start and was in a 2-for-32 slump that dropped his batting average to a season low .188 on May 27. The New York newspapers reported that Yankees owner George Steinbrenner wanted to trade the young center fielder. Yankees general manager Gene Michael purposely took his time trying to find a match. The delay turned out to be a blessing for the Yankees.

Williams found his hitting stroke at the end of May. He started his surge with a two-run homer off Mike Harkey on May 28, and two days later at Seattle he drove in the 200th run of his career. For the month of August, Williams hit .354, totaling 46 hits, the most in one month by a Yankee since Steve Sax had 47 in September 1991. During that surge, which lasted through the rest of the season's 119 games, he hit .332.

He missed only two starts in center field, and one was for a very important family matter. Williams had started in center field in 200 of the Yankees' previous 201 games, including 116 straight. He was scheduled to fly home to Puerto Rico on September 15, following the birth of his daughter Bianca, but the airport in Puerto Rico was closed because of Hurricane Marilyn.

He finally got home to see his family after a Sunday game against Detroit. The Yankees were off the next day, and Williams was to rejoin the team in Milwaukee. However, he failed to show up in time to start. "I got to the airport. I missed the plane. I got caught in traffic," said Williams, who finally did get to the ballpark for the game.

The birth of his daughter helped Williams celebrate a fine season. He batted .307 with 18 home runs and 82 RBIs. All were career highs.

That year, the Yankees won the wild-card berth in the American League, their first trip to the postseason since 1981. New York won the first two games of their playoff series against the Seattle Mariners. In Game 3 at Seattle, Bernie distinguished himself by hitting a home run from each side of the plate. He was the first major-leaguer to do so in the postseason, and the bat he used for that game is now enshrined in baseball's Hall of Fame in Cooperstown, New York.

The Mariners, encouraged by sellout crowds of 57,000 at the Kingdome, rallied to tie the best-of-five series at two games apiece. In the deciding Game 5,

Seattle won 6-5 in 11 innings, and the Yankees were finished for the year.

The 1995 season also was Don Mattingly's final year with the Yankees. The first baseman had been a tremendous influence on Williams.

"You hear about the 'Yankee way' at a young age in the organization, but I didn't really understand it," Williams said. "But it took only a week of watching Donnie—the way he carried himself on and off the field—to realize what being a Yankee is all about."

There is a mystique about the Yankees. You feel it the minute you walk into Yankee Stadium. So many great players have worn the distinct Yankee pinstripes, like Babe Ruth, Lou Gehrig, Joe DiMaggio, Roger Maris, Mickey Mantle, and Reggie Jackson. Players today are only a few steps from the history. Plaques honoring some of the team's all-time greats are in Monument Park behind the center field fence at Yankee Stadium.

The Yankees aren't cocky. They are professionals and they wear their pinstripes with pride. They project a confident image because of all the championships they have won. Every person who passes from the Yankee clubhouse through a tunnel onto the field sees a sign above that states: "I want to thank the good Lord for making me a Yankee." It is a statement by DiMaggio, and a sentiment all Yankees share.

Under Showalter, the Yankees had finished fourth in 1992, second in 1993, first in 1994 and second in 1995. Showalter decided to ask Steinbrenner for a long-term contract after the 1995 season. The

Yankees owner said no, and Showalter resigned. He would eventually join the expansion Arizona Diamondbacks as their first manager.

Steinbrenner, notorious for changing managers at a moment's notice, named Joe Torre the new Yankees skipper. It was the 21st managerial change since Steinbrenner purchased the team in 1973.

"I knew what I was getting into when I accepted this job," Torre said.

He had spent 18 years as a big-league player and 14 as a manager and had never gotten a World Series ring. This could be his chance.

CHAPTER FIVE
Playoff MVP

Manager Joe Torre was not the only new face in the Yankees' camp for the 1996 season. On Opening Day, only 14 players remained from the expanded 1995 roster. There were 15 new additions and four players on the disabled list when the Yankees kicked off the first season under their new manager. Among the new names were left-handed power-hitting first baseman Tino Martinez and right-handed pitcher David Cone. Bernie Williams was now a mainstay in center field.

Torre and the Yankees got off to a good start, and they overtook the Baltimore Orioles for first place in the American League East on April 30. New York held the top spot for 153 consecutive days, their longest stretch in first place since the 1976 season.

New York had led the AL East by as many as 12 games in late July, but that lead had dwindled to 2 1/2 games on September 15. All the Yankees had to do to clinch the division was win one of the games in a makeup doubleheader on September 25. They did so in a dominating way. New York beat the Milwaukee Brewers 19-2, the Yankees' highest scoring game in 34 years. It was an awesome display of power. The Yankees scored four runs in the first and added 10 more in the second to go ahead 14-1. It was the most productive first two innings in the club's 94-year history.

The Yankees also won the second game, 6-2. The Yankee Stadium crowd of 37,947 stood from the first pitch of the ninth inning of the opener to the last out of the nightcap, which ended with a flyout to Williams in center. After the catch, confetti poured out of the stadium's upper deck and the players celebrated in the infield surrounded by riot-geared police. The Yankees had won the East Division.

"It's a great feeling," Williams said at the time. "We battled hard all year."

Bernie was a key part of the team's success. He hit .305 with career highs of 29 home runs and 102 RBIs. The home run totals were the most by a Yankee center fielder since Bobby Murcer hit 33 in 1972. Williams became one of four players in the last 30 years to hit at least 13 home runs from both sides of the plate.

New York had to face the Texas Rangers in the first round of the playoffs, the division series. The Yankees got off to a bad start in Game 1, losing 6-2 in front of 57,205 disappointed fans at Yankee Stadium. The Yankees rallied in Game 2, winning 5-4 in 12 innings. Bernie got the team going in Game 3 with a first-inning home run and added a sacrifice fly in a 3-2 New York win.

Bernie powered a comeback in Game 4. In the 1995 division series against Seattle, he had distinguished himself by becoming the only player ever to hit a home run from each side of the plate in the postseason. He did it again against Texas in 1996. The Rangers had opened a 4-0 lead after three innings. The Yankees countered with a three-run fourth inning and added a solo homer by Williams in the fifth. Williams then turned around and hit a solo shot in the ninth and finished the series batting .467.

Reggie Jackson, the legendary Yankee player and Hall of Famer, earned the nickname Mr. October because of his postseason heroics. Bernie Williams was being called the nouveau Mr. October. He had hit three home runs in the four-game division series against Texas.

"I'm like a surfer," Williams said. "I'm just riding the wave. It's going pretty good right now. It has been a long time that I've waited to play at this level. I'm just having a lot of fun right now."

Next up for New York were the Baltimore Orioles in the American League Championship Series. The Yankees used an angel in the outfield to snatch a victory from the Orioles in a controversial Game 1. The Yankees trailed the Orioles 4-3 with one out in the eighth inning when shortstop Derek Jeter hit a long fly ball to right field. Jeffrey Maier, a 12-year-old boy from Old Tappan, New Jersey, stuck his glove over the right field wall of Yankee Stadium and appeared to deflect the ball. However, umpire Rich Garcia ruled that the ball had gone cleanly over the wall for a home run, meaning the Yankees had tied the game 4-4. "To me it was a magic trick because the ball just disappeared out of midair," Orioles right fielder Tony Tarasco said.

With the game tied and one out in the 11th inning, the switch-hitting Williams, batting right-handed against Orioles ace lefty Randy Myers, launched a 1-1 slider into the second deck in left field for a home run, setting off a wild home-plate celebration.

The Yankees went on to win the American League Championship Series 4-1. Williams earned Most Valuable Player honors in the ALCS, hitting .474 with two homers and six RBIs. "The whole club should get the MVP, from the bullpen to the lineup to the starting pitcher to the manager—everybody," Williams said. "We've been able to pull together as a team from Day One."

The 1996 Yankees were a veteran team, but reaching the World Series was still exciting. "It's indescribable," Torre said. "When you go through a career and you know how tough it is to do it, then you start getting close, you start to get excited. You've got to tell yourself, 'Don't get excited.'"

"Pretty unbelievable," said Yankees catcher Joe Girardi. "It's just like the United States in here. It's one big melting pot in this room. Guys coming from everywhere and we all seem to fit together."

But it was not going to be easy for the Yankees. Their opponent was the National League champion Atlanta Braves, who had one of the best pitching staffs in baseball. Atlanta had rallied from a 3-1 deficit in the National League Championship Series and outscored the St. Louis Cardinals 32-1 over the final three games to advance.

The Braves cruised easily in Game 1, winning 12-1 behind outfielder Andruw Jones and pitcher John Smoltz. Jones homered in his first two at-bats in the game. In Game 2, Greg Maddux shut down the Yankees 4-0, allowing six hits over eight innings.

The Series then shifted to Atlanta. The Yankees had come from behind all season and now they needed a rally. In Game 3, Williams broke a 1-1 tie with a two-run homer in the eighth inning to lead New York to a 5-2 win. In Game 4, Atlanta had opened a 6-0 lead entering the sixth inning when the Yankees scored three runs. In the eighth, Jim Leyritz hit a three-run homer off Mark Wohlers to tie the game 6-6, and New York scored twice in the 10th to even the best-of-seven series at 2-2. In Game 5, Andy Pettitte outdueled Smoltz to win 1-0, and the Series moved back to New York.

Bernie hit a two-run homer in the 8th inning at Fulton County Stadium in Atlanta, Georgia during game 3 of the World Series in 1996.

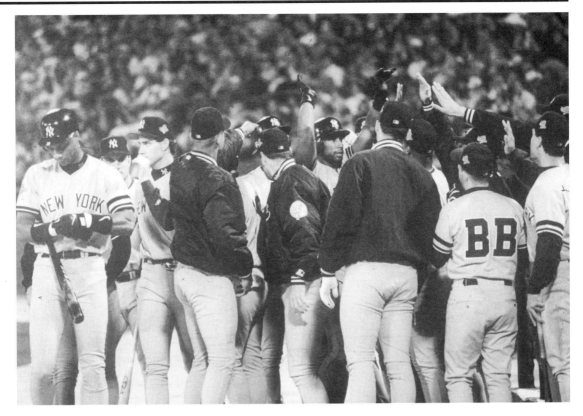

Torre had more to deal with than baseball that summer. His brother Frank was hospitalized and waiting for a heart transplant. On the eve of Game 6, Frank Torre received a new heart.

Joe Torre took a deep breath before getting the word from bench coach Don Zimmer that everything was OK.

"Zim says to me, 'Don't worry, this one is for Frank,'" Joe Torre said. "This is dreamland for me."

The Yankees had to beat Maddux, Atlanta's ace, for the championship. Maddux retired the first six batters before O'Neill doubled to right to lead off the third. With O'Neill on third and one out, Joe Girardi tripled

Bernie's teammates gave him high-fives for his game-winning two-run homer.

over the head of Marquis Grissom in center to score O'Neill and put the Yankees up 1-0.

Derek Jeter then singled to left over a pulled-in infield for the second New York run. Jeter stole second on Maddux's first pitch to Williams, who promptly singled him home to make it 3-0.

New York starter Jimmy Key lasted only 5 1/3 innings before the Yankees' dependable bullpen came on to shut the door. Atlanta's Chipper Jones doubled and advanced to third with one out in the sixth, but New York relievers David Weathers and Graeme Lloyd stranded him there. Yankees set-up pitcher Mariano Rivera threw two scoreless innings to hand it off to the closer, John Wetteland.

The Yankees clinched the championship with a 3-2 victory over Maddux and became the first team in history to lose the first two games at home in a World Series and then win four straight. It was the franchise's 23rd championship. Wetteland collected saves in all four wins to win the Series MVP award.

In 48 hours, Torre capped 32 years in baseball with receiving the good news that his brother was doing well after his heart transplant and that he had won a world championship.

"I've never been so happy. I never thought this would happen to me," Torre said.

"It really was a team effort," Boggs said. "On paper, there were three teams that were better than us: Baltimore, Texas and Atlanta. Of the four teams, we were probably ability-wise ranked fourth, but we found a way to win thanks to Jeffrey Maier and all the little things."

Following a crazy celebration on the mound, the Yankees went on a victory lap around the field to salute the delirious crowd of 56,375. Boggs got into the swing of things, jumping on one of the police horses and riding around with arms held aloft.

"I'm deathly afraid of horses," Boggs said later. "But I wanted to tip my hat to these fans. I've been on both sides of the fence now, and believe me, I'm walking on air."

Williams did not fare as well in the World Series against the Braves' vaunted pitching staff as he did in the playoffs. He hit just .167 in the six games. But he was able to enjoy what was truly a team win. And an emotional win, too.

"I look back at this World Series and the last month," Torre said. "I think it was all supposed to happen. Once we got here it seemed like nothing could stop us. A team like this is a rarity. This team wasn't concerned about numbers, only winning. We used all the ingredients. That's what glued us together. The whole thing was like some out-of-body experience; it really is dreamlike."

It was just the beginning.

CHAPTER SIX
Slumps Happen

Winning the world championship is one of the most thrilling things to happen to a ballplayer. It also is one of the most exhausting. Because of the New York Yankees' success in 1996, Bernie Williams was in demand to make appearances and capitalize on his newfound fame. His life became very hectic.

"I think I went to the most cities I've ever been to in my life in one week," Williams said. "Three days I was in New York, then for two more I was in L.A. and Hollywood, then for one night I went to Las Vegas, then the next morning I flew out to Miami, spent about five days there, then I came back and spent about a week here, then I went for a week for the Macy's parade in New York. It's been like that since we finished the season. It's been crazy."

It was even crazier in Bernie's homeland of Puerto Rico. The island had basked in its major-league heroes before, including Roberto Clemente and Orlando Cepeda. Williams and his fellow countryman Juan Gonzalez, who won the American League Most Valuable Player award in 1996, were toasted throughout the country.

"It's getting more and more difficult to walk around the streets," Williams said. "Everybody wants to get an autograph or a picture. Even the places where I used to go—my old high school, my old grade school—everybody kind of like goes crazy. They want me to sign everything."

Puerto Ricans had been able to watch Bernie and the Yankees on television. Cable television let them see most of Juan Gonzalez's home runs. In the past, the exploits of star players like Clemente and Cepeda were celebrated only in the newspapers the next day.

"For the first time since they have [had] the championship series, two Puerto Ricans took the big honors," said Osvaldo Hil, president of the Puerto Rican amateur baseball federation. "Here we were watching them doing it. We saw why they got the awards because they were so terrific. For a while in Puerto Rico, everybody was talking everywhere about baseball.

"People developed pride countrywide. Everybody feels more proud being Puerto Rican. One guy from a small island like this can become the best of all the good players. The whole island felt great because of their success."

Williams acknowledged that his life would probably never be the same in his homeland.

"It's a thing I have to deal with," said Williams, whose six postseason home runs and 15 RBIs led the Yankees to the World Series championship. "It's great to have the support. Juan and Carlos Baerga and Roberto Alomar have been living through this the past three or four years, and I never realized what they were going through. Now I'm going through the same thing. I guess I'll get some tips from them."

In 1996, Bernie had won his arbitration hearing and received a $3 million salary, a significant raise from his 1995 salary of $400,000. His agent, Scott Boras, had tried to get a multiyear contract prior to the start of the 1997 season, but instead Williams and the Yankees agreed to a one-year deal worth $5.25 million in February.

The Yankees started the 1997 season not only as the defending world champions but also as the team with the highest payroll at $57.1 million. It was time to play ball.

Bernie started the year well and batted .306 before the break. He joined the elite players when he was named to his first All-Star team. In mid-July, a strained hamstring sidelined him and he did not rejoin the Yankees until August 1. August was a great time for Bernie. He earned Player of the Month honors, hitting .395 in 29 games with eight home runs, one triple, 10 doubles and 23 RBIs. He finished the season driving in 33 runs in his final 34 games to reach the 100 RBI mark.

On September 28, Bernie hit his 100th career home run off Detroit's Greg Keagle. He finished the year ranked third among American League center fielders with a .993 fielding percentage and a .328 batting average, which ranked fourth in the league. He totaled 21 homers and 100 RBIs and hit for average from both sides of the plate. He started 127 games, all in center field, and his consistent play earned him his first Rawlings Gold Glove award, presented to the top defensive players in the game.

The 1997 Yankees compiled a 96-66 record—which was better than their 92-70 mark the previous year—but finished two games behind the Baltimore Orioles for second place in the American League East. New York reached the playoffs as the wild-card team and had to face the Central Division champion Cleveland Indians in the division series.

The Indians were a veteran ballclub and had reached the World Series in 1995, only to lose to Atlanta. In Game 1 against New York, Cleveland scored five runs in the first inning off David Cone. The Yankees rallied with three consecutive homers in the sixth by Tim Raines, Derek Jeter and Paul O'Neill but lost the game 8-6.

New York opened a 3-0 lead in Game 2 but this time the Indians rallied to win 7-5 and took a 2-0 lead in the series. Game 3 was played in Cleveland, and David Wells pitched a spectacular game for the Yankees, giving up one run on five hits over nine innings as

Not every call went Bernie's way.

New York won 6-1. O'Neill hit a grand slam in the game.

Cleveland came from behind in Game 4 to post a 3-2 win, scoring the game-winning run on an infield single in the ninth inning by shortstop Omar Vizquel. On October 6 the Indians clinched the series with a 4-3 win in front of 45,203 fans at Cleveland's Jacobs Field. Manny Ramirez hit a two-out, two-run double and Matt Williams added an RBI single in the third inning for the Indians.

Bernie Williams was kept in check through the five-game series. He started all of the games but hit just .118 with two hits in 17 at-bats and drove in only one run. In 1996, Williams had been the batting star in the Yankees' division series triumph over the Texas Rangers.

"Slumps happen," manager Joe Torre said of his star center fielder. "He came into this series as hot as anybody. We're all human. Nobody is pressure-proof. I think back to the '71 World Series. Willie Stargell couldn't buy a hit and Roberto Clemente was the star. They couldn't get him out. Then, in '79, Stargell was the star."

In Game 5 against the Indians, Williams flew out to left field to end the game and leave the potential tying run on second base. The Indians won 4-3 and advanced to the American League Championship Series. The Yankees were finished for the year. After the game, Williams sat and stared into space in the clubhouse, shell-shocked at what had transpired. It was one of the lowest moments in his life. Pitcher David Cone described his teammates as being "devastated."

"We expected to win the series," Cone said. "Not taking anything away from the Indians, but people were crushed. In the back of the plane, Bernie was a mess."

Losing to the Indians was difficult for the Yankees to accept.

"This really stinks," said New York catcher Joe Girardi. "As much fun as we had last year, this season is really empty. We came up short and it will be a long winter."

When Torre returned to New York after the Cleveland series, he spent the night on the couch in his Yankee Stadium office. The manager's home was being redecorated while the team had been playing in the postseason.

"My wife wasn't there and the house was inundated with paint," Torre said. "My thinking was that I would be in Baltimore [for the next round]."

Ten minutes after the Yankees-Indians series had ended, Yankees owner George Steinbrenner vowed his team would "win it next year."

It was a bold statement by the boss that the Yankees would have to live up to.

CHAPTER SEVEN
Winning It All

New York Yankees owner George Steinbrenner did not waste time trying to forget about his disappointment over the way the 1997 season had ended. In February 1998, he promoted Brian Cashman from assistant general manager to the top job. Just 35 days later, Cashman acquired second baseman Chuck Knoblauch from the Minnesota Twins in a trade for four players and cash. Knoblauch signed a four-year, $24 million deal with the Yankees. The spunky infielder would be the Yankees' first true lead-off hitter since Rickey Henderson batted first in pinstripes in 1989.

Cashman also signed hitting specialist Chili Davis and traded pitcher Kenny Rogers to Oakland for third baseman Scott Brosius. With Rogers gone, the Yankees' rotation included David Cone, Andy Pettitte, David Wells, Hideki Irabu and Ramiro Mendoza.

It was a difficult winter for Bernie Williams after the disappointing way the 1997 season had ended. He arrived at spring training in Tampa, Florida, in February 1998 ready to go. He also had a new contract. Williams and the Yankees had agreed to a one-year, $8.25 million deal. He had tried to get a multiyear deal but Steinbrenner wasn't interested. Bernie announced he did not want to talk with the team about a new contract until the season was over.

Williams' agent, Scott Boras, had not publicly stated a number for a multiyear contract, but he had compared his client to major-league outfielders Gary Sheffield and Sammy Sosa, who both averaged more than $10 million a season.

One thing Williams wanted to avoid was having his contract situation become a distraction. "This team is too good to have the season tarnished by Bernie Williams' contract situation," he said. "Hopefully, it will be a situation where we'll play so well that my contract situation will not be a matter of discussion."

Playing well is exactly what the 1998 New York Yankees did.

Yankees manager Joe Torre knew he had an owner who hated to lose. When the Yankees lost four of their first five games of the 1998 season, rumors started to circulate that Torre's job was

In 1998, Bernie signed an $87.5 million contract that will keep him with the Yankees until 2005.

in danger. Fortunately for Torre, his players did not like losing either.

The Yankees, who were never in first place for a single day in 1997, captured sole possession of first place in the American League East on April 21, 1998. It was a position they would not relinquish the rest of the season.

Williams started slowly and went 119 at-bats without a home run before he hit a two-run shot off Kansas City's Glendon Rusch on May 12. The next day, he hit his fifth career grand slam against Texas ace Rick Helling. Williams was named American League Player of the Month for May, batting .402 with seven homers and 27 RBIs.

On June 10 at Montreal in an interleague game, Williams slid awkwardly into third base and sprained his right knee. He would miss 31 games because of the injury. The Yankees were leading the American League East by 11 games at that point. The Bronx Bombers were incredibly balanced, with several players able to pick up the slack. Despite losing their No. 4 hitter, the team maintained its lead in the division and went 21-10 before Williams returned to the lineup.

Bernie came back strong. He compiled a 16-game hitting streak from July 31 to August 14, batting .365 during that stretch. On August 16, the 50th anniversary of Babe Ruth's death, Williams blasted a Ruthian-like home run into the upper deck in right field in the bottom of the ninth inning to lift the Yankees to a 6-5 victory over the Texas Rangers. The 401-foot home run capped a 4-for-5 day for Williams and enabled the Yankees to move back to 60 games over .500 with a 90-30 record and tie the 1944 St. Louis Cardinals as the quickest team to 90 victories.

Before the game, the Yankees had marked Ruth's anniversary with a moment of silence. Fittingly, the game featured six home runs and was decided by Williams' shot off reliever Xavier Hernandez in the famed "House That Ruth Built."

"I think he [Ruth] wouldn't have wanted it any other way," Williams said. "This is certainly the house that he built and it's a nice tribute to his memory. That's what baseball is all about. You come out, bottom of the ninth, tie game, and hit a home run like that. That's what dreams are made of."

Not every player can handle clutch situations. Bernie Williams can. He is able to block out the crowd noise and the pressure and the million other distractions when he stands at the plate. Williams did not really understand why he could do this until the summer of 1998 when his son, seven-year-old Bernie, was diagnosed with attention deficit disorder (ADD). Williams recognized the symptoms in both himself and his father.

"You sort of feel like you don't fit right, to some extent," Williams said. "You're always looked at as someone special. People would get everything that nobody else would get and they would miss everything else that everybody would get. I'm sort of like that. It's helped me a lot. I get into my own little world and I get like 'hyperfocus.'"

Although everyone has times when they feel hyper or say things that "just come out" or just can't pay attention, people with ADD have a problem with these things. For example, if a teacher says, "Get to work," a child with ADD may play with his or her pencil or stare out the window. They just can't concentrate on what they need to get done. Sometimes they act "spacy" because they are daydreaming. What is important to remember is that someone with ADD can be brilliant. Some people think Albert Einstein may have had ADD.

People with ADD have trouble paying attention to things that are boring to them. But if they love what they're doing, you can't tear them away. Bernie Williams loves baseball. He also loves music.

"Music gives me a vehicle to express myself in ways that I probably couldn't with words," said Williams, who doesn't consider ADD a handicap in any way. "I just think it's awesome."

Williams wanted to learn more about ADD, so he read a lot of books. "My dad's even worse," Bernie said. "He didn't know anything about ADD back then. You can work it to your advantage. It's just weird to explain. Some people with total deficit disorder, they are like dreamers and are totally spaced out. I feel like I'm sort of that way. But when they have to really concentrate on something, they just get hyperfocused and just block everything else out. I think, in that matter, it has really helped me in this game."

Not many people know that Bernie has ADD. It is not something that is listed on the back of his baseball card or something he likes to talk about. It is something he has learned to live with.

Williams could often be found playing his Fender Stratocaster guitar in the corner of the clubhouse. Before a game between the Yankees and Minnesota Twins at Yankee Stadium, rock star Bruce Springsteen visited Williams and even autographed his guitar. He wrote: "To Bernie, If you ever get tired of baseball . . ."

"He signed my guitar, so I have to get another one," said Williams, who did admit he prefers jazz to Springsteen's rock and roll.

There were plenty of things that could have distracted Williams in 1998. Would this be his last season in New York? What if his agent couldn't work out a new contract at the end of the season? Did Bernie want to stay with the Yankees? He was certain of only one thing: He wanted to perform well.

"I was under more pressure to perform this year than any other year . . . but every year I've been here, I've had to face some adversity and had different challenges," Williams said. "If you're going to play in New York, you have to be able to handle all that. Handle the pressure, handle the adversity and overcome it. I just wanted to give my best this year, and the fans who know my game will appreciate that, regardless of my contract."

It was Bernie's best season ever. Besides claiming the batting title with a .339 average, he hit 26 home runs and drove in 97 runs in 128 games. He was presented with his second consecutive Gold Glove, which is awarded to the top defensive player at each position.

The Yankees cruised through the 1998 season, winning a major-league-record 114 games. But the players knew that the record would mean nothing if the team did not win the world championship. They needed to win it all to be considered the best team in baseball. New York's first opponent in the division series was the Texas Rangers.

Before the playoffs began, the Yankees had to deal with unwelcome news. The day after the last regular-season game, New York outfielder Darryl Strawberry was diagnosed with a cancerous tumor on his colon and was scheduled to undergo surgery during the division series. Strawberry sent his teammates a video, pointing at them and yelling, "Do it!" The Yankees wrote Strawberry's No. 39 on their caps in support and did just as he told them, sweeping the Rangers in three games.

Williams struggled, going hitless in 11 at-bats against Texas. He returned to his batting champion form in the American League Championship Series against the Cleveland Indians. He led the team with a .381 average in the six-game series, including a 3-for-4 performance in Game 6 when New York clinched the title with a 9-5 victory before a rowdy Yankee Stadium crowd of 57,142.

The San Diego Padres were the only thing between the Yankees and another world championship. In Game 1 at Yankee Stadium, the Yankees scored seven runs in the seventh on a three-run homer by Chuck Knoblauch and a grand slam by Tino Martinez to win 9-6. Williams homered in Game 2, a 9-3 victory, and received a loud ovation from the fans in center field when he took his position. He waved back.

Third baseman Scott Brosius stole the show in Game 3 as the Series moved to San Diego. He hit a two-run homer in the seventh and a three-run blast in the eighth off Padres closer Trevor Hoffman to lead New York to a 5-4 come-from-behind victory. Andy Pettitte threw seven shutout innings in Game 4 as the Yankees posted a 3-0 win and captured their 24th world championship, the most titles by any team in professional sports.

With the win, Bernie Williams became the only player ever to win a batting title, Gold Glove and World Series in the same season. He now had two championship rings, and each had a different feel.

"We were heavy underdogs in 1996," he said. "We were playing the Atlanta Braves and everyone was saying so much about their pitching and their players. We were so underrated against them. And the way we went about it, too—losing the first two games and going to Atlanta and winning the next three and winning the last one here was just amazing. That made '96 very special. It was my first time in a World Series.

"Don't get me wrong—'98 was great, too," he said. "Any time you win a World Series ring is amazing. The fact that we were so dominating the whole year. We were the big dogs going into the Series, mowing down people and sweeping them and playing Cleveland and San Diego. It was more a thing that everybody expected us to win. Once we did it, the reaction was good, but it wasn't as great as '96. I think '96 was very special."

Winning the World Series quieted the Yankees critics. With their final 125-50 record, which includes the postseason, the Yankees played 75 games over .500 during the year that marked the 75th anniversary of the franchise's first world championship as well as that of the opening of Yankee Stadium. Of the 50 games New York did lose, all but 18 were decided by one, two or three runs. "I can't see anybody dominating the league the way we did," shortstop Derek Jeter says. "I mean, 125-50? That's ridiculous."

What was the magical moment of 1998?

"Winning the Series," Williams said. "From an individual perspective, it was watching [David] Wells throw his perfect game [May 17 vs. Minnesota]. Watching him deal from center field was awesome.

"I'd also have to say winning the batting title on the final day of the season," Williams said. "I knew I needed to get a hit, so there was a lot of pressure. When they put it up on the board that I had won it, the crowd went nuts and I had to go out for a curtain call from the clubhouse where I was just hanging out in my T-shirt, pants and shower thongs."

It was impossible for Williams to sum up the 1998 season in one word.

"It was a combination of both talent and chemistry," he said. "We definitely had the talent, but we also were all willing to put aside our personal goals and play as a team. There wasn't one guy who carried us."

Once the 1998 season ended, "It took me three days to pack when I went to the stadium because I kept forgetting things," Bernie said. "Every time I went back, I went to the field and took a long glance at the stadium. I had all these emotions about when I was there playing. Even though nobody saw me, it was very emotional."

The Yankees were special to Williams, but he still decided to file for free agency after the season ended. He could then solicit contract offers from other teams. The Yankees' only offer at season's end was $60 million over five years. The Boston Red Sox tempted Williams with a $91.5 million contract. The Arizona Diamondbacks dangled a $100 million package.

"I hope when Bernie makes his decision he takes that into mind, that it's a special thing here," O'Neill said of the Yankees mystique. "When you're talking this kind of contract, the long, long-term deal that Bernie is in line for, he has to realize there's no looking back. These people are good people, and great players. It's not often you have a chance to win, pretty much year after year. Every couple of years you're going to have a chance to win a World Series. You can't say that in too many other places."

Former Yankee great Reggie Jackson agreed. "I know what it meant to me when I played here," Jackson said. "I didn't know what it meant to me on the way here. When I was coming to New York, when I left Oakland, I had a chance to play in Baltimore. I had a chance to play in L.A., Montreal, all those places. I didn't really understand the stage here. I think if you're born on this stage, as Bernie was, you may not realize it's not like this everywhere else."

Williams was "born" into the Yankees system in 1986 when the team signed him out of Puerto Rico at the age of 17.

"It would be hard to imagine him not being in the pinstripes," Cashman said. "No other uniform would fit right."

His teammates had made their intentions clear way back on September 13. It was Bernie's 30th birthday, and his wife, Waleska, had thrown him a surprise party. It was a players-only party, and outfielder Chad Curtis had bought Williams a gift, which he put inside an old toothpaste box and wrapped.

"Oh," Bernie said when he opened the box. "A pen."

His teammates laughed. It was not the pen Bernie would use to sign his contract, but the message was clear. They wanted him back, at any cost.

Steinbrenner did not like the idea that the Red Sox, who were the Yankees' arch rivals, would take one of his star players. In early December, the Yankees and Williams finally reached an agreement, and Bernie signed a seven-year, $87.5 million deal with the team. It would pay him an average of $12.5 million a year.

Williams had been looking for both the security and the riches that a talented player deserved at that point in his career. But he admitted that he did not want to leave New York. The Yankees tradition meant the most to him. "I think the Yankees as an organization, as a baseball franchise, that's what I was really looking at," Williams said.

While he had considered signing with the Red Sox, Williams also thought Boston's interest would have had an emotional effect on its arch rival. "I think deep down—I don't think it would have been easy for the front office to let me go to Boston," he said. "I didn't see that happening without a fight."

Bernie was ecstatic about staying in pinstripes. "It came down to the fact that I wanted to be a Yankee," he said. "I wanted to remain a Yankee for most of my career."

CHAPTER EIGHT
DiMaggio's Choice

The Yankee pinstripes never looked so good to Bernie Williams as when he reported to spring training camp in Tampa, Florida, in February 1999. His new $87.5 million contract had not altered his approach to the game. "Fame, security, money, whatever, it's good — but it's not what really drives me as a player and I think that will never change," he said. "The fact is I'm a baseball player. That's what I love doing, that's what drives me."

The motivating force for the Yankees in 1999 was another world championship. First, the team had to survive an unusual spring. On March 8, Yankee legend Joe DiMaggio died. DiMaggio was known as the "Yankee Clipper" and he had played for the team from 1936 to 1951. A Hall of Famer, DiMaggio was revered by Yankee fans for his effortless talent and classy style of play. The team added a No. 5 patch on the sleeve of their jerseys in DiMaggio's honor.

Five days after DiMaggio's death, the Yankee players were shocked to learn that their manager, Joe Torre, had prostate cancer. Torre had to leave the team to undergo treatment and he put bench coach Don Zimmer in charge. The thought of losing their popular manager bothered the Yankee players. In mid-

March, Torre visited the team. He reminded the players that they needed to focus on baseball and not worry about him. "We have to prepare," Torre said. "The mental part is a big part of it. We need to get that going."

With Torre recuperating at home, the Yankees started the 1999 season in Oakland and lost the opener, 5-3. The Yankees then won seven games in a row to open a slim 2 1/2 game lead over Toronto in the American League East division at the end of April.

Bernie got off to a slow start. Entering the Yankees game May 3 against Kansas City, Williams had just four hits in his last 22 at-bats. But on that day, he hit a 417-foot, two-run homer to lift the Yankees to a 9-7 victory over the Royals. "I took a good swing and it was very satisfying because I haven't been hitting the ball in the air lately," Williams said. "It's the usual stuff. I have been pressing too much, pulling off and not waiting long enough. You name it and I have done it."

The team's spirits improved dramatically on May 18 when Torre was given permission by his doctors to return to the dugout to manage. It was the start of a big three-game series against the Yankees' rivals, the Boston Red Sox. However, Boston won two out of three games and regained first place in the division, a spot the Red Sox would not relinquish for 22 days.

In mid-June, Torre tinkered with the lineup to try to get some of the slumping players back in gear. Part of the switch involved moving Williams up from the No. 4 spot to No. 2 and dropping Derek Jeter from No. 2 to No. 3. The move produced immediate results. The Yankees won 13 of their next 17 games through

June 28. In nine games in the No. 2 spot, Bernie hit .476 (20-for-42) with five homers and eight RBI.

Williams was a joy to watch. He ran with an effortless grace in center field and was a powerful presence at the plate. "Bernie works hard at everything he does," said Yankee hitting coach Chris Chambliss. "I just try to make him aggressive because sometimes he gets too methodical and it slows him down. Bernie has a lot of talent. He can do a lot of things. He runs, he's got power, he does a lot of things well. When you're aggressive, you see all of that come out at once."

Williams has a deliberate routine before each at-bat. When he gets to the batters box, Bernie first lays his bat down across the front of home plate and notes the spot where the bat's knob lies. Then he draws a line straight back in the direction of the catcher from that spot. This helps with his foot placement. He doesn't want to step over the line. "He's trying to not dive too much with his front leg," Chambliss said of Bernie's routine. "I didn't teach him that. I remind him of it because I know why he does it."

Bernie was a little odd. He could often be found alone in his locker, playing one of his electric guitars. His teammates would tease him good-naturedly because he was very quiet, a little eccentric and very careful with his money. "Bernie's just different," Yankees designated hitter Chili Davis said. "He's a musician. Musicians aren't from this planet. They're 'Men in Black'-type guys. Baseball is a stepping stone-thing for Bernie. It just happens to be that he's good at it."

The Yankees were very good in June and put together a 17-9 record. On July 18 against the Montreal Expos, Don Larsen threw out the ceremonial first pitch at Yankee Stadium. Larsen had thrown a perfect game for New York in 1956. David Cone was pitching for the Yankees against the Expos, and he went out and duplicated Larsen's feat by throwing a perfect game in a 6-0 victory. Cone did not allow a walk or allow a single hit. It was one of the highlights of the Yankees' season.

There were also weird moments. With the bases loaded against Oakland pitcher Mike Oquist on August 9, Williams took ball three and then took about 10 steps toward first base as if he had drawn a walk. He had lost track of the count and thought it was ball four. Bernie got his first clue that something was not right when Jeter didn't move from first base. Williams stopped and turned to look at home plate umpire John Shulock who waved him back. Bernie smiled and sheepishly returned to home plate.

Oquist then threw a fastball and Williams hit it into the right field seats for a grand slam to open an 8-0 lead. It was one of a major league-record five grand slams hit that day. The Yankees went on to win 12-8 for their sixth consecutive win.

"Only Bernie," said Yankee catcher Jorge Posada. Only Bernie could forget the count and then hit a grand slam on the next pitch. Williams laughed about his mistake afterward. "If anybody on the team was going to do that, it was bound to be me, because I'm the goofy one," he said.

Bernie also was the hottest hitting Yankee at that point of the season. He was batting .532 with runners in scoring position since the All-Star break and had 30 RBIs in his last 26 games. "It's tough to pitch around him since he is a switch hitter," Yankees teammate Tino Martinez said. "That just helps us all see more men on base. He's what separates us from a lot of teams. He gives us that depth that we need. It's easy to notice that when he's not there."

Bernie paced the Yankees in August, batting a team-high .384 with seven homers and 34 RBIs. He did so despite a sore left shoulder that had bothered him since late June. The injury changed Williams' perspective regarding the game he loved. "I'm preparing myself to play every game as if it could be my last," Williams said. "Basically, I've realized that this is a precious time and that you have to enjoy it while you can."

The pain finally became too much and on September 8, Bernie left the team in Kansas City to return to New York to undergo a magnetic resonance imaging (MRI) test on his left shoulder. Williams threw with his right arm, so the shoulder only bothered him when he hit. The diagnosis from the test was that Bernie could play the rest of the year. He would just have to endure the pain.

The Yankees had other concerns. Boston was closing the gap in the AL East. New York lost its fourth straight game September 13, a 2-1 decision to Toronto. Williams was hitless in the game and grounded into a double play in the ninth inning. "He feels like he's letting people down," Torre said of Bernie, who had three extra base hits in his last 25 games.

September 13 also was Bernie's 31st birthday. That night, he and his wife Waleska went to dinner at a Toronto restaurant to try to celebrate. It was tough for Bernie to enjoy the evening. "It gets to him, it really does," Waleska said. "I can always tell when he's in a slump because he doesn't say anything." Waleska was not only his wife but also his biggest fan, his coach, his psychologist and his friend. "I have to go through it all with him," she said.

The next day, Bernie gave himself and the Yankees a belated present when he hit a game-tying grand slam off Toronto's Billy Koch in the eighth inning. Paul O'Neill hit another slam in the ninth to lead the Yankees to a 10-6 victory over the Blue Jays. "It takes one swing like that to put a smile on your face," Torre said of Williams' home run, his first in September.

"You could see him after the game and how good he felt about it," Cone said of Bernie, who ran around the clubhouse giving everyone high fives. "He was the most elated guy in the clubhouse. That's highly unusual for Bernie. He was talking about it being a defining moment for us. You know how deep a thinker Bernie is. You know what that could mean."

After the game, Waleska joked that she was going to change Bernie's birthday to September 14 and that she planned on the two of them dining at the same restaurant they had the night before. "I'm not saying I'm superstitious, but it can't hurt us," she said.

Whatever she did, it worked. The next night, Bernie hit his 150th career home run, a two-run blast, to give the Yankees a 6-4 victory over Toronto. Torre was ecstatic. "He takes his responsibility so personally and seriously that you love it when he is rewarded like that," the manager said.

The slump and sore shoulder were all forgotten. The grand slam was Williams' second this season and seventh of his career. More important, the come-from-behind win reminded the Yankees what they could do. "It feels great whenever you hit a grand slam because it doesn't happen that often," Bernie said. "But to do it at that time, to shift the momentum of the game, was great. For the past week we couldn't put everything together and then — bang — it just happened."

His teammates were relieved. "Bernie's our big gun, there's no doubt about it," O'Neill said. "He takes that role and he relishes that role and he excels in that role."

The Yankees clinched the Eastern Division on September 30 with a 12-5 victory over the Baltimore Orioles in the second game of a doubleheader. It was a significant game for Bernie who got two hits to reach 200 that season for the first time in his career. He and Jeter became the first Yankee teammates to each have 200 hits in the same season since DiMaggio and Lou Gehrig did so in 1937. Williams finished the regular season batting .342, third best in the American League, with 202 hits, 115 RBIs, 116 runs and 100 walks — all career highs — and hit 25 homers.

But the only month that counts for the Yankees is October when the playoffs start. New York, which finished with the best record in the American League at 98-64, had to face the high-powered Texas Rangers in the first round for the third consecutive year.

Bernie is happy to be playing for the World Champion New York Yankees. Almost every game puts a smile on his face.

Game 1 of the American League Division Series was played October 5 at Yankee Stadium. Before the sell-out crowd of 57,099 could settle into their seats, Bernie was struggling with himself. "I thought I was going to have a terrible night," he said. "I was sleepy and dragging a little bit and it was cold. All throughout batting practice, I was like, 'Wow, I don't know how I'm going to get through this.'"

Then, Bernie heard public address announcer Bob Sheppard's distinctive voice.

"Something happened when they said the lineups," Williams said. "I started hearing the anthem and something inside of me just woke up and I said, 'It's time to play.' I said, 'You just have to go out and play hard, you've got to wake up. This is the postseason. This is not the regular season anymore.'"

Williams dominated Game 1. He made an impact even before his first hit. With runners at first and second in the Rangers third inning, slugger Juan Gonzalez hit a looping liner that Williams tracked down in right-center field and made a sliding catch to preserve a 1-0 Yankees lead.

Then he went to work with his bat. Bernie was down 0-2 in the count in the fifth inning against Texas starter Aaron Sele. He worked the count to 3-2 and then hit a double off the center field wall to drive in two runs. Bernie added a three-run homer in the sixth and hit an RBI single in the eighth as the Yankees opened the best-of-five series with an 8-0 victory. "Bernie is a special person, a special talent," Torre said. "If he was making 10 cents, he'd be the same person."

The Yankees' talented pitching staff held the high-powered Rangers to one run in three games as New York swept the series and clinched on October 9 with a 3-0 win. Bernie batted .364 in the series. His first-step quickness helped him cover a lot of ground in the outfield. "Once he gets going, there's not too many people that are as fast as him," Jeter said of Williams. "That's how you win games, with pitching and defense, and our pitching obviously has been unbelievable but we've played great defense as well."

Bernie did not join his teammates in the clubhouse to celebrate the sweep over Texas. He knew what was ahead. "It's one of those things, you enjoy the moment — and certainly you shouldn't take it for granted," he said. "But at the same time, we look ahead and try to get to the next step."

Boston was next. The Red Sox, who won the AL wild card, had upset Cleveland in five games to advance. The best-of-seven American League Championship Series opened at Yankee Stadium on a rainy October 13. The two teams were tied 3-3 going into the bottom of the 10th inning. O'Neill had made the last out in the ninth so Williams knew he would be leading off the 10th. He had been in this situation before. In the first game of the 1996 ALCS against Baltimore, Bernie had homered off Randy Myers in the 11th inning. "That was all I was thinking about the innings before, when Paul grounded out (to end the ninth)," Williams said. "It was kind of like a setup for the same situation I had in 1996. But I tried to keep my mind off it because it was a different pitcher, a different team, but the setup was sort of the same. I mean, what are the chances of it happening twice? Not too much."

Rod Beck started the 10th for the Red Sox. His first pitch to Williams was inside and a called strike. The scoreboard clock showed one minute before midnight. The next pitch was right where Bernie wanted and he drove it to straightaway center field. The ball disappeared behind the blue wall for a game-winning home run and a 4-3 Yankee victory.

Williams pumped his arm as he saw the ball clear the fence. He lept onto home plate with both feet and then fell into the arms of his teammates who had run from the Yankees dugout to congratulate him.

"I don't know if it's something about Game 1s, I just think it's something about Bernie Williams, period," Tino Martinez said. "Every time we need a big hit, Bernie is going to get it. Every time we need a great defensive play, Bernie is going to give it to us. Every time we need a home run, Bernie is going to get it."

The Yankees won 3-2 in Game 2 to take a 2-0 lead but Boston romped 13-1 in Game 3 behind the masterful pitching of Pedro Martinez. It would be the only game the Yankees would lose in the entire play-offs.

Bernie went 3-for-5 to help New York bounce back and post a 9-2 win in Game 4 and Orlando Hernandez pitched a decisive game October 18 as the Yankees clinched the AL pennant with a 6-1 win.

The Bronx Bombers were headed back to the World Series. The fall classic was nearly a New York, New York affair as the New York Mets battled the Atlanta Braves for the National League pennant. But the Braves edged the Mets in six games to advance, setting up a rematch of the 1996 World Series. The Yankees had lost the first two games of that series before winning 4-2. This time, the Braves never really had a chance.

The Yankees thoroughly outpitched and outplayed Atlanta to complete a four-game sweep and complete the drive for their 25th world championship on October 27 with a 4-1 victory in front of 56,752 cheering fans at Yankee Stadium. The Bronx Bombers went 11-1 in the playoffs and became the first team to sweep back-to-back World Series since the 1938-39 Yankees did so.

Game 4 was an emotional game for O'Neill, who received word earlier in the day that his father, Charles, who had been ill, had died. O'Neill still played that night but with a heavy heart. When the final out was recorded, O'Neill joined his teammates briefly on the field for the celebration, then ran into the dugout with tears streaming from his face.

Later that night, Bernie was passing through a stadium walkway in a joyous mood, shaking hands and slapping backs. Then he saw O'Neill. The two men embraced. No words needed to be said.

The Yankees operated as efficiently as a machine. But the players were human and they bonded together, beginning with DiMaggio's death and Torre's illness. The tragedies seemed to make them a stronger unit. "Sometimes, I think we just cared a little more than the other team," O'Neill said.

The Yankees won 12 consecutive World Series games, dating back to the 1996 season, to tie an all-time record set by the 1927-'28-'32 Yankees. Torre and his team had captured baseball's top prize three of the last four years. The 25 world championships are the most by any team in any sport. The Yankees could clearly boast that they were the Team of the Century. "Some of the kind of stuff that goes on in Yankee Stadium, it seems like it's almost a fairy tale," said pitcher Andy Pettitte.

The Braves had pitched around Bernie, who batted .231 in the four games. But this was a World Series he could truly enjoy. After all the controversy at the end of the 1998 season about whether he would return to New York or leave via free agency, Williams could celebrate. Both he and the Yankees were committed to winning and to each other — at least through the 2005 season. And Williams had Joe DiMaggio to thank for that.

Yankee owner George Steinbrenner had visited DiMaggio three days before he died and one of the things the "Yankee Clipper" told Steinbrenner to do was to sign Williams. Bernie already had a new contract by that time but now Steinbrenner had the blessing of the legend who once played the same center field at Yankee Stadium.

The city of New York held a parade to honor its champions. A father and son wearing identical Bernie Williams jerseys and blue Yankees caps were part of the thousands of spectators lining the procession route.

"I've been a Yankee fan all of my life," said 7-year-old Joshua Williamson. "Bernie's my favorite because we like him. He can really hit and he's the best outfielder."

And he's a key part of the World Champion New York Yankees.

MAJOR LEAGUE STATS

YR	TEAM	G	AB	R	H	2B	3B	HR	RBI	BB	.AVG
1991	NYY	85	320	43	76	19	4	3	34	48	.237
1992	NYY	62	261	39	73	14	2	5	26	29	.280
1993	NYY	139	567	67	152	31	4	12	68	53	.268
1994	NYY	108	408	80	118	29	1	12	57	61	.289
1995	NYY	144	563	93	173	29	9	18	82	75	.307
1996	NYY	143	551	108	168	26	7	29	102	82	.305
1997	NYY	129	509	107	167	35	6	21	100	73	.328
1998	NYY	128	499	101	169	30	5	26	97	74	.339
1999	NYY	158	591	116	202	28	6	25	115	100	.342
2000	NYY	141	537	108	165	37	6	30	121	71	.307
TOTALS		1237	4806	862	1463	278	50	181	802	666	.304

CHRONOLOGY

1968	Born September 13, in San Juan, Puerto Rico

1968   Born September 13, in San Juan, Puerto Rico

1985   Signed as a non-drafted free agent, September 13, on 17th birthday

1988   Won first minor league batting title, hitting .335 for Class A Prince William

1990   Married Waleska February 23 in Puerto Rico

1991   Made major league debut, July 7, against Baltimore.

1992   Son Bernie Alexander born September 23

1993   Spent first full season in major leagues, starting the year as Yankees leadoff hitter

1994   Daughter Beatrice Noemi born April 20

1995   Daughter Bianca born September 14; Became the first major league player to homer from both sides of the plate in a post-season game

1996   Hit 29 home runs, most by Yankees center fielder since Bobby Murcer hit 33 in 1972

1997   Won first Gold Glove award for top defensive player and selected to first All-Star team; hit 100th career home run September 28 at Detroit

1998   Signed seven-year, $87.5 million contract with a club option for an eighth year with Yankees on November 25; contract extends through the 2005 season; First player ever to win a batting title, Gold Glove and World Series championship in same season; won AL batting honors with .339 avg

1999   Reached 200 hits on September 30 for first time in career; joined Derek Jeter as first Yankee teammates to have 200 hits in the same season since Lou Gehrig and Joe DiMaggio did so in 1937

INDEX